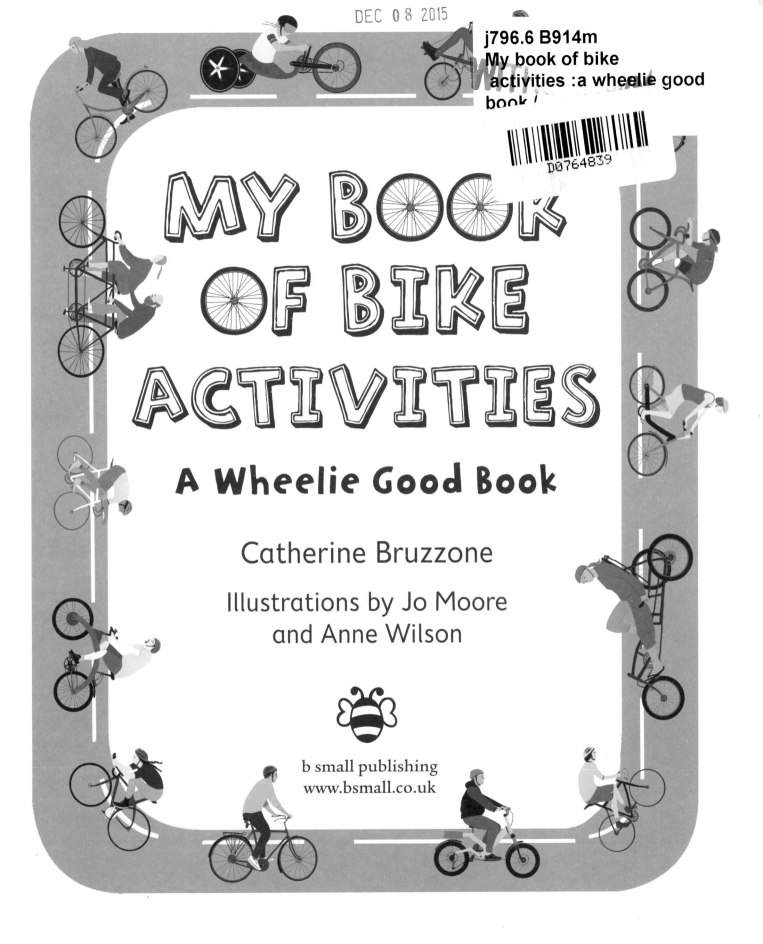

MY BOOK OF BIKE ACTIVITIES

A Wheelie Good Book

Catherine Bruzzone

Illustrations by Jo Moore
and Anne Wilson

b small publishing
www.bsmall.co.uk

Which is which?

Match the bike to its name. Fill in the labels from the list opposite.
Find out more about these bikes on pages 30 to 47.

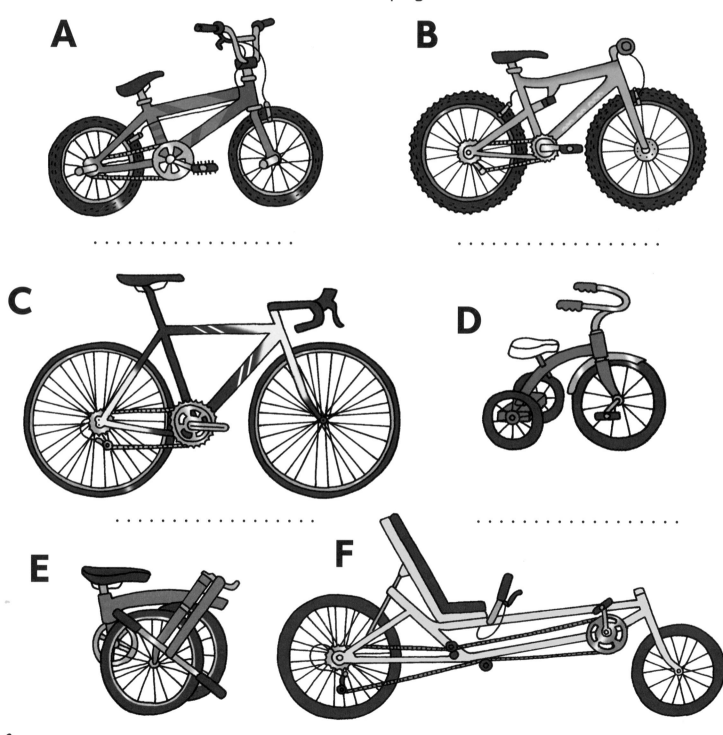

A
. . . .

B
. . . .

C
. . . .

D
. . . .

E
. . . .

F
. . . .

penny-farthing • recumbent bike • BMX bike • city bike • MTB or mountain bike • racing or road bike • tandem • folding bike • tricycle

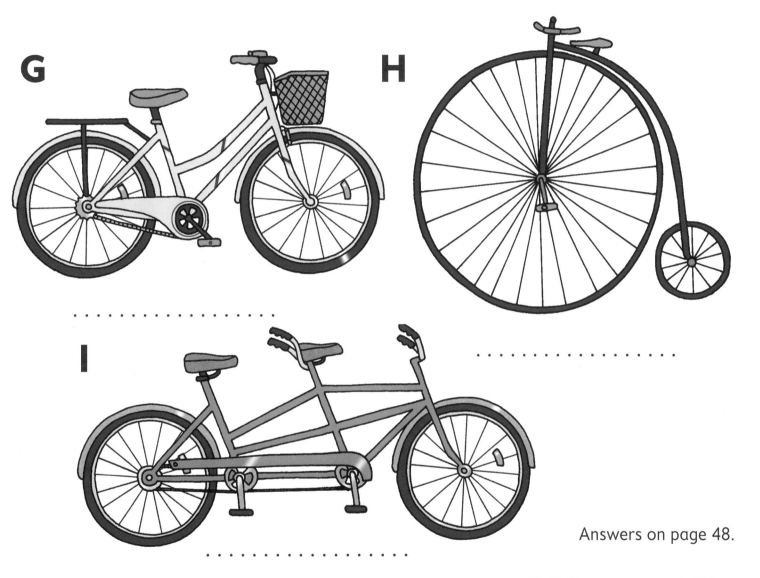

G . . . .

H . . . .

I . . . .

Answers on page 48.

ECO GRAFFITI

Mud stencils are created by graffiti artists who want to send a message but also respect the natural world. This muddy bike symbol will wash away in the rain. Maybe before it disappears it will encourage someone to go cycling?

Spot the difference

Look at these four scenes of the MTB track at the Olympic Games.
Can you spot 10 differences on page 5? Answers on page 48.

USE YOUR HEAD

Mountain bike riders can't stop without using their head. Not literally! A rider must use the rocks, dips, climbs, twists and turns on the path to help control their speed. Simply slamming on the breaks would make them fly over the handlebars.

Know your bike

Can you add the missing labels?

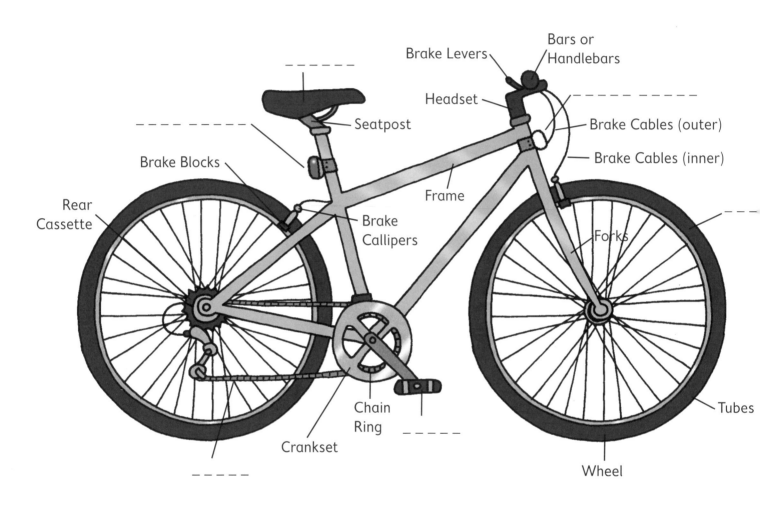

Brake Levers

Bars or Handlebars

Headset

Seatpost

Brake Cables (outer)

Brake Cables (inner)

Brake Blocks

Frame

Rear Cassette

Brake Callipers

Forks

Chain Ring

Crankset

Tubes

Wheel

Answers on page 48.

PUFF, PUFF

It's important to keep your bike tyres well pumped up. This makes it easier to pedal, helps prevent punctures and gives your tyres a longer life.

(See page 16 for how to mend a puncture.)

Whoooosh!

On 29 December 2013, Guy Martin pedalled his bike at 112.94 mph (miles per hour) along the hard packed sand on a beach in Wales and beat the British record for speed on a bicycle following a vehicle.

The world record is held by Dutch cyclist, Fred Rompelberg. In 1995, he cycled at 268.831 kph (166.94 mph) along a dried up salt lake in Utah, USA. The speed limit on a British motorway is 70 mph, so that's more than twice as fast!

How did they do it? First they trained hard to build up their strength. Then their bikes were specially built with a very high gear. Finally they cycled behind a speeding vehicle. This shielded them from the air and saved a lot of effort. It's called slipstreaming.

Fred rode behind a dragster car and Guy behind a racing lorry. First they were pulled. Then they unhooked the tow and pedalled like mad. This is very, very dangerous as they were extremely close to the back of the vehicles. There are more amazing speed records on a bike on pages 23 and 25.

Wheelie madness

There are 15 bikes on this page. Can you find them all?

BMX for beginners

Here are two starter BMX tricks or stunts.
If you give them a try, follow these basic safety rules:
- wear a helmet, gloves and sturdy shoes
- don't try them on or near a road
- take them slowly at first: practice, practice, practice makes perfect.

Bunny hop

Start slowly.

Lift up your front wheel.

As it falls, pull up your back wheel.

Practise going over an object first to give you the right movement.

Foot jam endo

Start slowly.

Take one foot off the pedal and jam it on your front tyre just behind the fork.

This will flip the back of your bike up.

Keep the pedals even and either leave the other foot on the pedal or lift it off and balance on the front tyre.

Make sure your bike doesn't lift too high at first. Try it on grass and expect a few tumbles!

Can you tell the story of this sequence of pictures?

_____

_____

_____

_____

_____

_____

_____

_____

_____

_____

Hidden cycle words

Can you find these words in the wordsearch?

Answers on page 48.

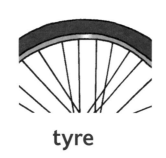
lock

tyre

gears

brakes

wheel

spokes

pedal

bell

saddle

basket

K W U A W P E D A L
A E T C H A I N G V
S P O K E S N B T B
U S Z B E X F R Y A
H A N D L E B A R S
S D J U N C E K E K
K D W P D M L E K E
C L O C K P L S B T
G E A R S R H F B J
A F Q U K W P U M P

chain

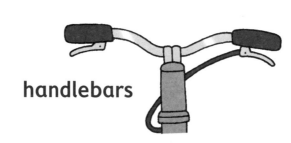
handlebars

pump

World's longest bike?

This **LONG** bike was built by Indonesian villagers out of rusting iron pipe. It has just two wheels and is ridden by one person but needs a team of people to get it in position – and it's best if there are no bends on the road. Amazingly, it isn't the longest bike in the world. The Indonesian bike is 13.41 m (44 ft) but a Dutchman, Mijl van Maers Werkploeg built a bike measuring a massive 35.79 m (just over 117 ft). That's as long as one and a half tennis courts!

World's tallest bike?

Richie Trimble of Los Angeles USA thinks his T**ALL** bike is the tallest in the world. He built it himself and he looks down on to the tiny people below from a height of 6.16 m (just over 20 ft).

Which bike wins this race?

The history of the bicycle

1817
Draisine, Dandy or
Hobby Horse

1860s
Velocipede or
Boneshaker

1870s
penny-
farthing

FINISH

1
2
3
4
5
6

Answers on page 48.

You can find out more about some of these bikes on pages 21, 36 and 42.

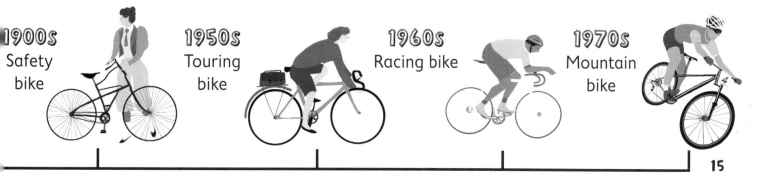

1900s
Safety
bike

1950s
Touring
bike

1960s
Racing bike

1970s
Mountain
bike

15

How to mend a puncture

Although modern tyres are almost puncture-proof, these instructions may come in handy. Practice makes perfect.

Before you start - you'll need:

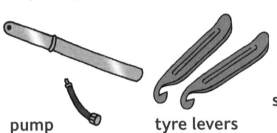

pump

tyre levers

small piece of chalk

tube of glue

sandpaper or grater

rubber patch

1 Turn your bike upside down.

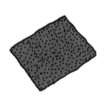

2 Turn the tyre slowly and look for whatever has caused it to go flat: a sharp stone or a nail. Pull this out very carefully if you find it.

2 Take off the wheel. You will need to release the brake blocks first. The back wheel is more difficult because of the gears. Ask for help the first time you do it.

4 Make sure there is no more air in the tyre. Usually you can do this by pressing the end of the valve.

5 Take the tyre off the rim. Hook the levers on to the spokes as you go round. When you've removed a short section, pull off the rest of the tyre. Be careful not to pinch the inner tube.

6 Pull out the inner tube very carefully still making sure not to pinch it. Check all round inside the tyre to make sure there is nothing still causing the hole.

7 Pump up the inner tube.

8 Look for the hole. Listen for the air escaping or dip it in water. Dry the tyre if it is wet.

9 Mark the hole very clearly with a cross. Use chalk if possible. Let the air out again.

10 Rub the rubber around the hole with sandpaper to roughen the surface.

11 Spread the glue over the roughened surface. Let it dry. Repeat this once more.

12 Peel the backing carefully from the patch. Don't touch the sticky part. Put the patch on to the glued area and press down hard.

13 Start to put the inner tube back in the tyre. Put the valve through the valve hole in the rim first.

14 Gently push the rest of the inner tube under the tyre. Make sure it doesn't get twisted or pinched.

15 Fold the tyre back on to the rim, pressing carefully with your thumbs. Push the valve up to keep the inner tube out of the way.

16 Put the wheel back on the bike. Ask for help to reconnect the brakes and the gears (back wheel). Make sure the wheel is straight and tighten the nuts well.

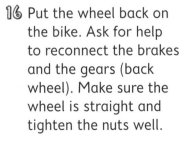

17 Pump up the tyre again.

17

Pick of the peloton

Look carefully at the Tour de France peloton on the opposite page. Then see if you can spot these details.

Seven green helmets

Nine pink helmets

Seven black cycle shoes

Eight pale blue lycra suits

Nine yellow T-shirts with red stripes

Seven green cycle shorts

Peloton

This is a French word that means 'pack' or military 'squad' and is used in cycling to describe the riders who bunch together during a road race. By keeping close to each other, they can reduce their effort. The riders in front create a slipstream behind them, an area with much less pressure, so the riders behind don't have to pedal so hard. The riders in the middle of the group save the most energy. The riders all change position in the peloton, taking turns to save energy. To win the race, they need to break out of the peloton...but this means using a LOT of extra energy so it's very hard.

Chain links

How many bicycle chain wheels can you count on this page?
Now colour in the patterns. Answers page 48.

The Dandy Horse or Draisine

In 1815, a German nobleman called Baron Drais von Sauerbronn was very worried about the terrible results of a huge volcano eruption that had spread dark ash all over the world. It blotted out the sun and caused the failure of the crops and death of many horses. In those days, horses were the main means of transport, at least for rich people. So, in 1817, the Baron invented a vehicle that was a mix of a horse and a carriage and it wouldn't need to be fed!

The riders had to push this Dandy Horse or Hobby Horse along with their legs so it was more like a game than a practical way to travel. In fact, in a short time the volcano ash disappeared, horses came back into fashion and Baron Drais's invention was abandoned. But it wasn't entirely forgotten and 150 years later, someone had the clever idea of adding pedals to the front wheel and a brake for the back wheel – the modern bicycle had arrived.

Hill too steep?

The city of Trondheim in Norway has a solution. This city has the highest number of cyclists in Norway but it also has a lot of hills. So they've installed a bicycle lift to help cyclists up the steepest hill in town. To use the lift, riders put one foot on the moving belt and balancing on their wheels, they're pulled to the top of the hill. Can you invent a useful piece of technology to help cyclists?

Bike bus

A bike bus keeps you fit, safe and is a great way to get to school. You cycle in a group, led by an adult with another adult following along at the back.

Use the descriptions of the young cyclists below to organise them into the correct order in their 'bike bus'. Write their names and numbers under their pictures. Then colour in the bike bus below with your own choice of colours. Answers page 48.

A   B   C   D   E   F   G

_____   _____   _____   _____   _____   _____   _____

1 Brenda is a parent. She is wearing black gloves and red boots.

2 Alice has blond plaits and blue trousers.

3 William has a red jacket and green boots.

4 Sam has blue gloves and a yellow helmet

5 Louise has an orange jacket and purple boots.

6 Robert has a blue helmet and brown boots.

7 Luke is a parent. He is wearing a red helmet and a black jacket.

Allez, allez!

Unscramble these names to discover the three most famous cycle races in the world.

ROTU ED ENRFAC

OIRG A'TALIDI

ETVUAL A SNEAPA

These names are in three languages. Which languages are they?

Clue: 'allez, allez' means 'go, go' in French and is the cry used by racing fans around the world as they cheer their cycling stars on, especially up the high mountain sections.

Answers page 48

The Flying Scotsman

In 1993, Scotsman Graeme Obree beat a world cycling speed record on his bike called 'Old Faithful'. He had to cycle for an hour as fast as possible around a velodrome. He built his bike himself using washing machine ball-bearings for the pedals when he saw how fast a washing machine could spin. The shape of the bike and his position were quite different from most racing bikes. He later built another bike using recycled parts, including an old saucepan.

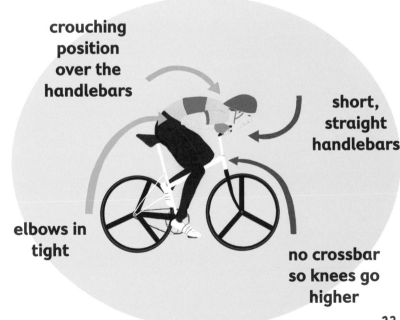

crouching position over the handlebars

short, straight handlebars

elbows in tight

no crossbar so knees go higher

23

Cycle quiz

1 **A bicycle made for two is called:**
a a tandem
b a modem
c a diadem

2 **Which of these men is a famous cycle racing champion?**
a Edward Elgar
b Eddy Merckx
c Eddie Murphy

3 **A bike with three wheels is called:**
a a bicycle
b a tricycle
c a unicycle

4 **How much carbon dioxide emissions could you save if you use a bike instead of a car to go 10 miles?**
a 4.5 kilos **b** 1 kilo **c** 3 kilos

5 **The bicycle mechanics who built the first aeroplane to fly successfully were called:**
a the Marx Brothers
b the Everly Brothers
c the Wright Brothers

6 **A 'keirin' is**
a the name of a Japanese bicycle
b the name of a motor bike that leads sprint cyclists round a velodrome track
c the bike part that attaches the wheel to the bike

Answers page 48.

Spot a cycle symbol

Look out for cycle symbols on the roads or on road signs.
Keep a count of any that you spot near your home or when you are away.
Take photos and see how many different ones you find.

Cycle track on mountain road in France

The symbol for the Triathlon in the Olympics

Recycle your bike
Many organisations will recycle bikes and donate them to people who need them

What do you think this sign is for?

Can you design your own symbol?

Volcano rider

Frenchman Eric Barone has the world record for hurtling down a volcano at 107 miles per hour in Nicaragua, Central America. Just as he hit the speed record, he had a terrible crash but luckily he survived. He also went even faster down an icy mountain in the French Alps to beat the world record on snow, speeding at 138 mph. Before he beat these records, Eric was a stuntman, acting as a stunt double in films for Sylvester Stallone and Jean-Claude Van Damne. (Don't try this at home!)

25

Brrrr!

This beautiful bicycle is sculpted entirely from ice.

You could have a go at making a mini-ice bike yourself.
You'll need to freeze a block of ice at least the size of a brick. Look at a picture of a bike.
Wear gloves, work very quickly with a sharp tool like a skewer (take care!).

All-year-round cycling

If you live in a very cold climate, you don't want to give up cycling in the winter. Here are some great ideas for bikes that you could use on ice.

Can you design your own?

Load it up!

In many parts of the world, motorbikes, cars and lorries are very expensive so bicycles are the way to get around even if you are carrying a heavy load.

1 Add 2 more bricks to this load. Then double the total load.
How many bricks?

2 Take 6 bricks away from the load. Then divide it by 2.
How many bricks?

3 Divide the number of bricks by 3. Then add 6 bricks.
How many bricks?

Answers page 48.

Back to the future

These strange, futuristic bikes might never be built but the designers really thought hard about their shape, their materials and how they would be used.

As this bike is built with flexible material, everything folds into the circular frame. Very neat!

This bike has a cool transparent roof to protect the rider from the rain.

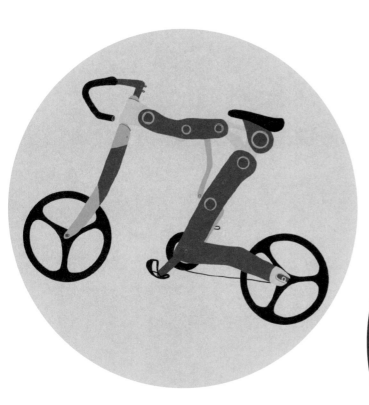

This bike is designed to bend and fit people of different heights.

Can you design a bike for the future?

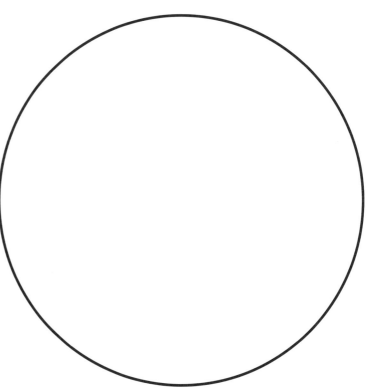

You can carry this bike up a mountain in your rucksack. Err... wasn't the idea of the mountain bike that you should ride it up the mountain?

And what about the cycle lanes of the future? They could be along a river...or maybe suspended up in the air? Where would you put them?

BMX

BMX stands for Bicycle Motorcross. BMX racing is an extreme sport. BMX riders go on dirt tracks, ramps, half pipes or just use them as their regular bike. There are two types of BMX bikes:

1    2

freestyle or stunt bike   **dirt jump/racing bike**

These bikes are lightweight and strong with knobbly tyres.

Your turn...
draw your own BMX
bike and customise it.

Velodrome

Velodromes are special tracks for very speedy bike racing. They are usually indoors, are an oval shape and have steep banks and a curve at each end.

The riders can go as fast as 85 kph (52 mph) and they have no brakes! To slow down you pedal backwards.

In a race you just have to keep the speed up. If you slow down, the bike falls over.

Like road racers, velodrome team racers ride very close to each other to take advantage of the slipstream (see page 18).

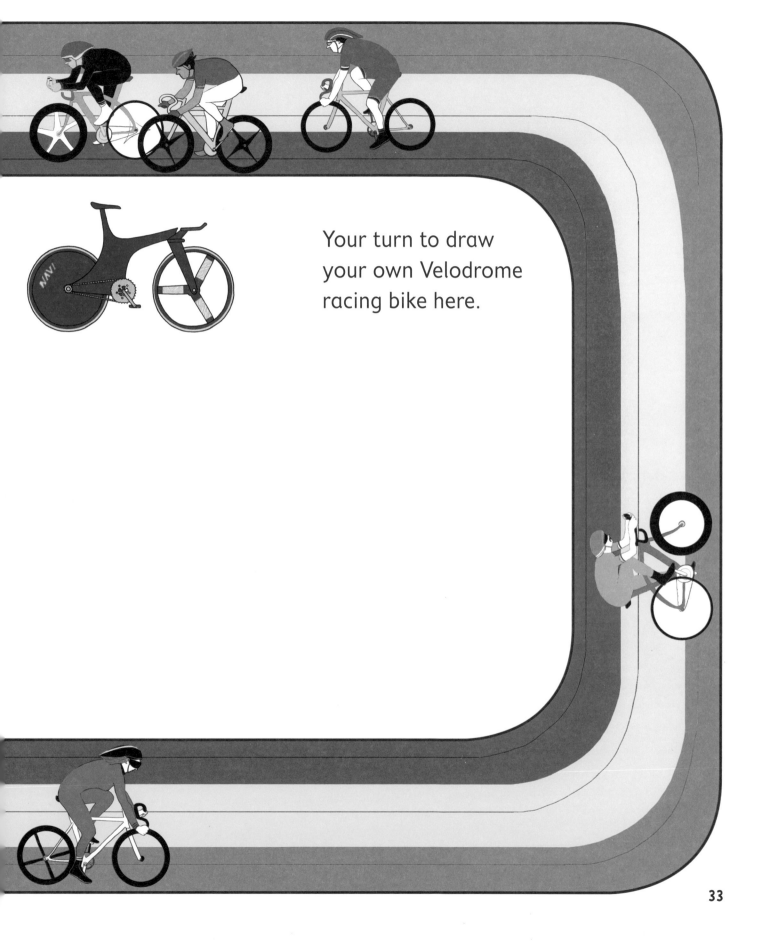

Your turn to draw your own Velodrome racing bike here.

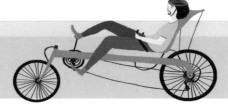

Recumbent

'Recumbent' means 'lying', 'flat' or 'resting'.
Instead of sitting up on the saddle, riders of a recumbent
bike are lying down but they're not resting! Recumbent
bikes go faster than upright bikes because they're more
aerodynamic (not so much drag from the air).

Recumbent bikes can be mountain bikes, racing bikes,
tandems and tricycles. Differently-abled cyclists can use
specially adapted recumbent bikes. So, for example, if they
can't use their legs, they can power the bike with their arms.

Your turn. Design your own recumbent bike here.
Look at all the different bike designs round the edge of the page.

Penny-farthing

It may be hard to believe but penny-farthings were the speedy bikes of their day. They were difficult and dangerous to ride but this made them popular with rich young men, even though it was common to fall over the front of the handlebars. Also called 'High Wheelers' or 'Ordinaries', they coped with the rough, rutted roads of Victorian England where they were invented. If you want a thrill, you can still buy and race penny-farthings today.

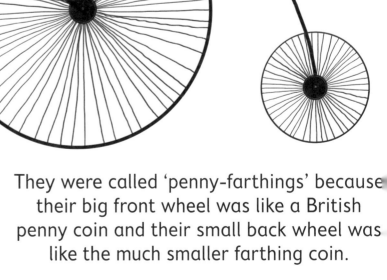

They were called 'penny-farthings' because their big front wheel was like a British penny coin and their small back wheel was like the much smaller farthing coin.

Your turn. Can you add the rider to this bike?

Tandem

This is a bicycle made for two and was invented not long after the penny-farthing. Cyclists have to pedal against the air or the 'wind resistance'. Tandems have about the same wind resistance as a single bike so they can go faster with less effort, especially on the flat or downhill. Uphill the riders must pedal carefully together.

Even small children can help pedal when they're the 'rear rider', the rider at the back of a tandem.

Now your turn.
Tandems come in lots
of shapes and sizes.
Design one
yourself here.

Electric bike

Isn't an electric bike just a small motorbike or moped?
No, the difference is that the electric bike can also be pedalled.
So in most countries you don't need a driving licence to ride
one but you aren't allowed to go too fast.

The first electric bike was made in 1895 in the USA so they're almost
as old as the penny-farthing. They are a great help uphill and against
the wind. They are also 'greener' than a car or motorbike but heavier
than a normal bike and you need to re-charge the battery.

Can you draw an electric bike? Invent your own design.
Lots of electric bikes are home-made and look very strange!

Racing bike

Racing bikes or 'road bikes' are used for races like the Tour de France.
They are high-tech machines and very expensive.
Everything from the handlebars to the tyres is designed for speed.

The bikes always have drop handlebars so the rider can crouch down and reduce wind resistance.

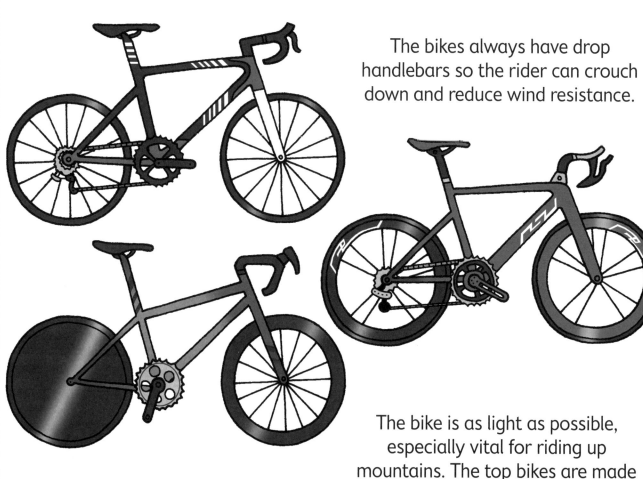

The bike is as light as possible, especially vital for riding up mountains. The top bikes are made from carbon fibre, a special material also used in planes and rockets. It is very light and strong - perfect for a racing bike.

Add a racer to this bike. Check back to page 19 and look at the riders going round the velodrome on pages 32 and 33 and round the edge of these pages. What colours will your racer wear?

Monowheels and unicycles

These unusual bikes only have one wheel! The monowheel has one big wheel and the rider sits inside it. The big wheel is driven by smaller wheels that go round the inside, pressing on the inner rim. The rider has to lean the whole wheel over to change direction.

Unicycles are much simpler and the rider sits on top.
They developed from penny-farthings. They are popular in circuses and can even have several wheels, one on top of another!

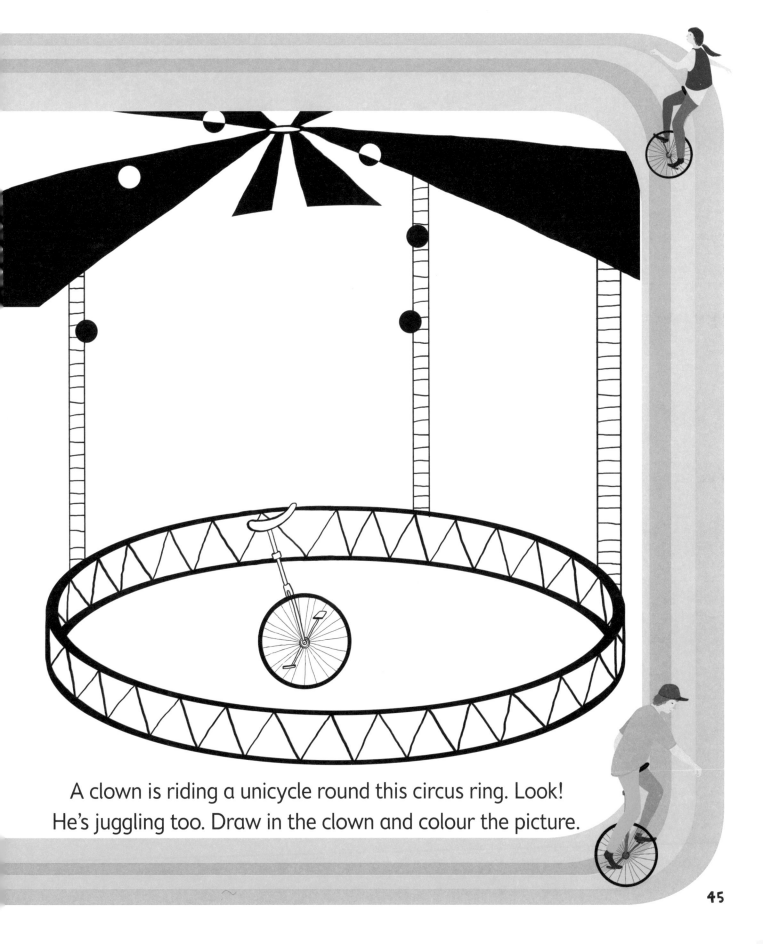

A clown is riding a unicycle round this circus ring. Look!
He's juggling too. Draw in the clown and colour the picture.

Cool city bike

This bike is designed for riding slowly round town.
It has mudguards and a chain guard to keep your clothes clean,
a comfy saddle and a shopping basket.

If you want to stop and nip into a shop, you
can prop it up on a stand. It also has big
bright lights for riding safely in the dark.

Add the saddle, mudguards, lights and
basket to this bike and the rider.

Answers

pages 2-3 – A: BMX, B MTB or mountain bike, C racing or road bike, D tricycle, E folding bike, F recumbent bike, G city bike, H penny-farthing, I tandem.

pages 4-5 – Top left: white sleeves to yellow sleeves, no sunglasses to sunglasses, bike number changes, number 7 to number 1. Top right: green frame to red frame, no pocket to pocket, red sock to blue sock. Bottom left: missing Olympic ring, missing cyclist. Bottom right: missing sun, green shorts to orange shorts

pages 6-7

pages 12-13

```
K W U A W P E D A L
A E T C H A I N G V
S P O K E S N B T B
U S Z B E X F R Y A
H A N D L E B A R S
S D J U N C E K E K
K D W P D M L E K E
C L O C K P L S B T
G E A R S R H F B J
A F Q U K W P U M P
```

pages 14-15 – the bike with the green jersey

page 20 – There are 20 chain wheels.

page 22 – A = 6 Robert, B = 3 William, C = 7 Luke, D = 2 Alice, E = 4 Sam, F = 1 Brenda, G = 5 Louise

page 23 – Tour de France/French (Tour of France in July), Giro d'Italia/Italian (Tour of Italy in May), Vuelta a España/Spanish (Tour of Spain in August-September).

page 24 –

1 = a: a tandem; a modem is a device that converts a digital signal of a computer to an analogue signal of a telephone and so links the computer to the internet; a diadem is a crown or headband worn by a royal person.

2 = b: Eddy Merckx was a Belgian cyclist who won the Tour de France and Giro d'Italia 5 times each and is considered to be the greatest professional racing cyclist ever. Eddie Murphy is an American film actor and Edward Elgar is a British classical music composer.

3 = b tricycle, tri is from the Greek (treis) and Latin (tres) for three; bi is the Latin word for double or two and uni is from 'unus', the Latin for one.

4 = a: 4.5 kilos; most car trips are made within 10 miles of home. If we used bikes instead of cars, think how we could save fuel and reduce air pollution.

5 = c: brothers Wilbur and Orville Wright were American bicycle mechanics who invented and built the 'flying machine' that made the first flight on December 17th 1903; the Marx Brothers were American comedy stars and the Everly Brothers American pop singers.

6 = b: 'keirin' comes from the Japanese word for 'racing wheels' and this strange bike leads the racers around the track for a few laps. When it moves out of the way, the cyclists sprint to the finishing line.

page 27 – 1 = 40, 2 = 6, 3 = 12

Published by b small publishing ltd.   Text and illustrations © b small publishing ltd. 2015   1 2 3 4 5 6 7 8 9 10

British Library Cataloguing-in-Publication Data: A catalogue record for this book is available from the British Library.

Illustrations: Jo Moore and Anne Wilson   Design: Louise Millar   Editorial: Catherine Bruzzone and Sam Hutchinson   Production: Madeleine Ehm
Printed in China by WKT Co. Ltd.   ISBN 978-1-909767-69-0
Please visit our website if you would like to contact us: **www.bsmall.co.uk**